HEADLINE SERIES

No. 308   FOREIGN POLICY ASSOCIATION   Fall

U.S. Information Policy and Cultural Diplomacy

Introd.... 3

1 Origir
   and Ir 9

2 The C
   for the ..17

3 Confli ..36

4 The C
   and Ir ..46

   Talkin ..60

   Readin ..62

Cover Desigr $5.95

PRINTED IN U.S.A.

The Author

FRANK NINKOVICH received his Ph.D. from the University of Chicago. He is the author of *The Diplomacy of Ideas: U.S. Foreign Policy and Cultural Relations, 1938–1950, Germany and the United States: The Transformation of the German Question Since 1945*, and *Modernity and Power: A History of the Domino Theory in the Twentieth Century*. He has also written numerous articles on the role of culture and ideology in U.S. foreign relations. He is currently a professor of history at St. John's University in New York City.

The Foreign Policy Association

The Foreign Policy Association is a private, nonprofit, nonpartisan educational organization. Its purpose is to stimulate wider interest and more effective participation in, and greater understanding of, world affairs among American citizens. Among its activities is the continuous publication, dating from 1935, of the HEADLINE SERIES. The author is responsible for factual accuracy and for the views expressed. FPA itself takes no position on issues of U.S. foreign policy.

HEADLINE SERIES (ISSN 0017-8780) is published four times a year, Spring, Summer, Fall and Winter, by the Foreign Policy Association, Inc., 470 Park Avenue So., New York, N.Y. 10016. Chairman, Paul B. Ford; President, Noel V. Lateef; Editor in Chief, Nancy Hoepli-Phalon; Senior Editors, Ann R. Monjo and K.M. Rohan; Editorial Assistant, June Lee. Subscription rates, $20.00 for 4 issues; $35.00 for 8 issues; $50.00 for 12 issues. Single copy price $5.95; double issue $11.25. Discount 25% on 10 to 99 copies; 30% on 100 to 499; 35% on 500 and over. Payment must accompany all orders. Postage and handling: $2.50 for first copy; $.50 each additional copy. Second-class postage paid at New York, N.Y., and additional mailing offices. POSTMASTER: Send address changes to HEADLINE SERIES, Foreign Policy Association, 470 Park Avenue So., New York, N.Y. 10016. Copyright 1996 by Foreign Policy Association, Inc. Design by K.M. Rohan. Printed at Science Press, Ephrata, Pennsylvania. Fall 1994. Published February 1996.

Library of Congress Catalog Card No. 95-83910
ISBN 0-87124-168-4

Introduction

THE United States Information Agency (USIA) specializes in "public diplomacy," the promotion of communication between peoples as opposed to governments. Although the contrast with traditional diplomacy is clear, public diplomacy as a concept is quite fuzzy. It can refer to nationalist or internationalist objectives; to propaganda or the free exchange of ideas; to base or disinterested motives. It can use any or all of the varied media by which human beings communicate; it can target many different segments of public opinion; and it involves the government, the private sector, or both in varying mixtures. Finally, while at times public diplomacy has been kept at arm's length from foreign policy, on occasion it has been tied very closely to international diplomacy.

Many of these contrasts are inherent in the USIA's programs and organizational structure, which show two faces to the world: the cultural and the informational. Whereas the cultural programs emphasize exchanges of persons and ideas that have lasting effects on relatively small numbers of people, the overseas information programs have focused on the mass media. But these differences in means are less significant than their ends. The cultural-exchange programs are internationalist, concerned with promoting long-term mutual understanding between peoples. The information programs, by contrast, are in the nationalist tradition: largely one way in direction and more political in thrust.

As examples of cultural diplomacy in operation, one could point to the many American scholars visiting foreign countries at government expense to teach and conduct research and, reciprocally, the foreign scholars and students sojourning in the United States; concert tours made by Benny Goodman's band, the New York Philharmonic and other American musical groups to the former Soviet Union; or paintings of American artists being exhibited overseas. To illustrate the information programs, one might cite a soap opera beamed to Havana by Radio Martí; Voice of America (VOA) broadcasts to China; the organization of an American pavilion at an international trade fair; the USIA's "Wireless File" of speeches and documents for the use of foreign news organizations; or a transnational teleconference between reporters and officials on an important issue. More recently, computers and digitized transmissions have opened up new means of communication, as high-tech "resource centers" replace the traditional book-based libraries abroad run by the United States Information Service (USIS), as the USIA is known overseas.

Culture or Information?

The line separating the government's cultural and informational activities is not clearly marked. The sending and receiving of information is always shaped by culture, while culture is changed by information. Are books and movies informational or cultural? When American embassies arrange tours for distinguished guest speakers or when a foreign labor leader or promising young politician visits the United States as part of an international visitors' program, these activities straddle the divide between culture and information.

What role do these programs play in the conduct of American foreign policy? How have they contributed to the achievement of national objectives? These are not easy questions to answer. While the U.S. government has settled permanently (if not altogether comfortably) into the role of superpower, its involvement in cultural and informational affairs has continued to strike many observers as a questionable activity. Although cultural diplomacy has been part of U.S.

foreign policy since before World War II and informational programs have existed since 1942, Americans have never felt fully at ease with either. Never has there been unanimous agreement on their propriety or usefulness. By contrast, France, Germany and the Soviet Union jumped unblushingly into cultural diplomacy and propaganda activities in the 1920s. Actually, French cultural policy goes back at least to the nineteenth century, and one can also find many examples of cultural diplomacy in classical antiquity. If these activities have been accepted in a matter-of-fact way by other nations, why should they be so problematic for Americans?

Part of the answer lies in the continuing power of the myth of American exceptionalism—the belief that America enjoys immunity from the historical misfortunes that have plagued Europe. The United States has often been reluctant to adopt the values and practices of diplomacy pioneered by the European nations. Espionage and intelligence, balance-of-power thinking, elite policymaking ("Cabinet diplomacy"), secrecy in diplomacy and large standing armies in peacetime were long alien to American thinking on foreign affairs. The realist principle of the primacy of foreign policy has never found a wide following in this country. Not surprisingly, then, the emulation of cynical propaganda practices has always been considered un-American. Even the more benign and aboveboard cultural practices of other nations, those of the semiprivate British Council created in 1934, for example, have not been accepted as worthy models for this country.

This ideological resistance has deep historical roots in Americans' liberal conceptions of the proper role of government. In the United States, the terms conservative and liberal distinguish, somewhat confusingly, between two branches of liberal political thought: nineteenth-century laissez-faire and the "new liberalism" of the twentieth century. American conservatives ("old" liberals) tend to favor minimal government and free-market economics. Liberals ("new" liberals) are more willing to propose state intervention to deal with various problems.

When it comes to public diplomacy, both viewpoints profess intellectual and cultural freedom while differing on how to promote such freedom. Liberals have tended to favor an active government role in cultural relations while showing less enthusiasm for one-way informational diplomacy. At the same time, they have been suspicious of state interference in intellectual freedom. Conservatives, while preferring to rely upon the private sector, have accepted public diplomacy when warranted by national security concerns, while casting a jaundiced eye at government promotion of culture. Public diplomacy has been criticized from each point of view for being ineffective or too political.

Unlike Europe, where the omnicompetence of the centralized state has been a matter of tradition, in the United States the federal government's adoption of new responsibilities has tended to come only in the aftermath of perceived failures in the private sector. In matters of social and economic security, regulatory activities and responsibility for management of the economy, Washington has taken the reins only as a last resort.

In a nation where federal control of culture has always been a taboo, it was only during Franklin D. Roosevelt's New Deal in the 1930s that the government began to play a cultural role, and gingerly at that. As activities initiated by private organizations came to appear inadequate, the baton was passed to government, which expanded these programs and shaped them to its own purposes. The subsequent history of the cultural and informational programs shows that their institutional birth did not confer legitimacy. The government's programs have continued to be dogged at every step by doubts and second thoughts about the propriety of linking public policy with the promotion of ideas. This sniping, coming from both the left and right and inspired by one ideological facet or another of America's liberal tradition, has subjected public diplomacy to a continuous cross fire.

With their emphasis on the communication of ideas and images and the promotion of international understanding, government informational and cultural activities may appear at first sight to be unrelated to the conventional foreign policy concern with national security. Ideas and symbols are about communication, whereas power suggests the impossibility of mutual understanding. To be sure, traditional diplomacy is also a form of communication, but it would take a most extraordinary envoy to negotiate in the belief that agreements are based on common values. Instead, diplomacy has sought to arrive at accords that are based on power and interest. This long-standing belief in power as the foundation of international relations also implies the need to resort to force when agreement on presumably vital issues is unobtainable. Thus, when France's King Louis XIV (1643–1715) had engraved on the muzzles of his cannons "the last argument of kings," he was declaring in the least subtle way imaginable that war was the ultimate form of communication when words failed—as, at some point, they always did.

American Hostility to 'Official Culture'

The widespread belief that diplomacy is about power, combined with an underlying suspicion of the state as potential Big Brother, has produced a chronic apprehensiveness about government playing an active role in the promotion of ideas. The absence in this country of a Ministry of Culture, a commonplace organ in other lands, is indicative of an aversion to "official culture." Americans, with their deeply rooted hostility to the political control of ideas, have never been entirely comfortable with a tight governmental link to culture and information.

The effectiveness of these programs has also been a divisive issue. Do they work? Liberals tend to question the values and priorities of the information program, while conservatives often fail to see the point of cultural exchanges. Apart from the ideologically motivated criticisms, there exists considerable confusion about what these programs are supposed to do.

Even if this issue of effectiveness were settled, some critics would argue that the programs were simply duplicating functions performed by the private sector. The United States is, after all, the world leader in the manufacture and distribution of images and its advertising skills are unsurpassed. Hollywood, American television programs, the recording industry and performing artists are all part of a media colossus that provides immense foreign exposure for American culture. The United States leads the world in the number of book titles published. Although only a small proportion of citizens have passports, Americans have always traveled abroad in large numbers. Conversely, the United States is increasingly a desirable venue for foreign travelers fascinated by the wide open spaces of the West, Disneyland, New York City and Hawaii. With market forces operating on such a vast scale, government efforts can seem puny and redundant by comparison.

Criticisms and problems have often bubbled up from within the government itself. Time and again the informational and cultural programs have been accused by Congress of being wasteful. And, despite their absorption into the foreign policy apparatus, there has always been a nagging problem of organizational fit, with the result that these activities have never found a comfortable bureaucratic home. Although culture and information have long been joined administratively, their coexistence has always been uneasy. Last but not least, advocates of the programs have never been able to demonstrate convincingly where they fit into foreign policy strategy as a whole.

In the cold-war struggle against communism, which was in part a conflict of ideas, cultural exchanges and information were given the benefit of the doubt. With the end of the cold-war era, the ebbing of the ideological crisis provides an appropriate occasion for reconsidering their place in foreign policy and, more broadly, in foreign relations. A review of their history should help clarify the kinds of practical and ideological difficulties under which they labor. Once that background is understood, it should be possible to discuss the pros and cons of their relationship to American diplomacy. To foretell, the author's conclusion is that the programs are important and ought to continue, but for reasons different from the national-security arguments so often advanced.

1

Origins of U.S. Cultural and Informational Programs

THE STORY of American cultural proselytizing begins early in the nineteenth century, when missionary societies offered educational programs as a way of attracting potential converts. In the Near East and in China, schools featuring modern subjects and methods of instruction were opened. So successful were these private educational initiatives that the cultural results often wound up overshadowing religious aims. In contrast to the other powers in China, whose interests were primarily commercial and strategic, the United States by the turn of the century was the leading cultural power.

These religiously inspired efforts were secularized by the great philanthropic foundations created early in the twentieth century. In 1910, the Carnegie Endowment for International Peace, under the leadership of Columbia University President Nicholas Murray Butler, began to fund exchanges in the conviction that cultural differences lay at the root of international conflict. The creation of a new international public opinion—what Butler called an international mind—seemed to offer the only long-range solution to the problem of war. "Our troubles began at the Tower of Babel," observed Butler. "When language was multiplied and men were dispersed, the problem of organizing the world had its beginning."

Other philanthropic organizations, realizing that culture was closely tied to education, began to fund activities more seriously related to its transmission. In 1921, for example, the Rockefeller Foundation created a world-class medical school in Beijing, China, less from a desire to heal than to sow abroad the scientific mind-set that was the source of Western progress and power. According to President Raymond Fosdick, the aim was "to make over a medieval society in terms of modern knowledge." More typical of activities in the educational and cultural fields than this tightly focused program was the John Simon Guggenheim Foundation's funding, beginning in the 1920s, of two-way Latin American exchange fellowships as a way of fostering "commerce of the mind, of spiritual values." Other foundations, Rockefeller included, were soon funding fellowship programs of their own.

In 1919, the foundation-sponsored Institute of International Education was created to systematize and coordinate the complex details of what was a fast-growing but uncoordinated network of educational exchanges. Its founder, Stephen Duggan, was a convinced internationalist. He believed that there existed "a unity among men which transcends differences in the forms of government, but to know it and to understand it they must be brought together." Although the United States had failed to join the League of Nations after World War I, within the United States an enduring enthusiasm for nongovernmental internationalism found expression in numerous informal cultural ventures. Under the auspices of scholarly organizations like the American Council of Learned Societies and the American Council on Education, the United States sponsored a national affiliate of the League of Nations Committee on Intellectual Cooperation.

Until the mid-1930s, this system of privately funded and organized educational and cultural relations remained, for the most part, quite satisfactory to all concerned. That is not to say that there had been no governmental involvement. The earmarking of some of the Boxer Indemnity funds (a $333 million penalty exacted from China for its antiforeign uprising of 1900) for the education of Chinese students in the United States was only one example. During World War I, under the auspices of the Committee on Public Information (CPI), an ad hoc propaganda organ run by George Creel, the government launched experimental cultural and informational programs in a number of countries. However, the CPI's *domestic* activities proved to be too successful for its own good. Having whipped up an anti-German hysteria in the United States and an unrealistic expectation of a postwar international utopia, it left a sour taste in the mouths of many when the sober postwar morning after arrived.

The relatively brief period of American belligerency and the ruthlessness with which Congress dismantled the wartime agencies immediately after the armistice cut short any possibility that the CPI might take permanent root. Other nations were less hesitant to create official organs to regulate educational interchange. The French, accustomed to viewing their culture as a political resource, formally integrated *les relations culturelles* into their Ministry of Foreign Affairs in the 1920s. The British, for their part, created the British Council in response to the expanding propaganda efforts of the fascist powers.

Americans Oppose Government Role

For Americans, there seemed no need at the time for direct governmental involvement. The heavy hand of the state, it was feared, might easily choke off the free flow of ideas necessary to create a transnational human community. Worse yet, the politicization of information and culture might lead to a power politics of ideas, a facet of policy that the totalitarian powers were actively exploiting. In Latin America, for example, the Germans funded libraries, German-language instruction, exchanges of students and professors and other activities aimed at fortifying Nazism. In Germany's Third Reich, cultural attachés were political operatives in disguise, while the press and radio propaganda of Joseph Goebbels exemplified most chillingly how ideas could be perverted in the service of foreign policy.

In mid-decade the United States had retreated into the storm cellar of isolationism, but by the late 1930s the looming threat of expansionist totalitarianism, especially from Nazi Germany and militarist Japan, prompted a revival of internationalism. According to Secretary of State Cordell Hull (1933–44), the political and economic breakdown of the decade was "complemented by the breakdown of the commerce of mind and culture." As a companion to its Good Neighbor Policy in Latin America, the Administration of Franklin D. Roosevelt (FDR, 1933–45) began to promote cultural exchanges with the aim of creating hemispheric solidarity against the Axis (Germany, Italy, Japan). A precedent for a federal role in culture had only recently been created by the WPA (established in 1935 as the Works Progress Administration and renamed Work Projects Administration in 1939), which put unemployed artists, intellectuals and writers to work. By 1938, increasingly concerned by the harmful effect that the German propaganda machine was having on public opinion in Latin America, the U.S. State Department established a Division of Cultural Relations.

Taking this step did not mean that the government intended to enter the propaganda business. Far from it. The officials responsible for creating the Division of Cultural Relations viewed the agency as only a limited extension of private activities and renounced any desire to control cultural exchanges. The guiding idea was public-private partnership, not federal control. The expectation was that even funding would continue to come primarily from the private sector so that federal money would not tarnish the nonpolitical luster of the program.

To prevent contamination, the cultural programs were divorced from the doings of the State Department's policymaking divisions. Advisory panels drawn from cultural institutions in the private sector charted policy; the division would only "facilitate" and "coordinate" by serving as a clearinghouse. Though Americans believed that the nation had more to give than to receive in matters cultural, especially vis-à-vis Latin America, they nevertheless accepted unfettered cultural exchange as an article of faith.

Wartime Departures from Tradition

World War II was a watershed period in the evolution of both cultural and informational policies. The fire wall separating politics and cultural diplomacy was breached time and again. In Latin America, the Office of Inter-American Affairs, created in 1940 and headed by Nelson A. Rockefeller, launched a bevy of new cultural programs whose scope far exceeded the limited initiatives of the philanthropic pioneers. Energized by a spirit of wartime license and a budget that reached $60 million by 1943, this agency strove to interpret the United States to its Latin American neighbors. With once-scarce scholarship funds now flowing freely, sizable numbers of Latin American students began to enroll in U.S. universities. Visits by distinguished leaders and public opinionmakers were subsidized and aid to more than 200 U.S. schools in Latin America was provided. Cultural attachés began to appear on the rosters of American embassies overseas.

In China, the Open Door policy had always been, at bottom, a commercial and cultural policy directed toward the modernization of China. This emphasis on modernization took a more political turn during the war when cultural personnel stationed in China, increasingly upset with the backwardness, dictatorial methods and political ineffectiveness of their ally, argued forcefully that cultural relations should be used as an instrument for liberalizing the oppressive Kuomintang (Nationalist) regime of Chiang Kai-shek. Although FDR ultimately sided with Chiang, the episode demonstrated the uncomfortable degree to which cultural interference could be driven by political and ideological motives.

While cultural programs were expanded, the greater wartime departure lay in the field of information policy. The creation of an imposing bureaucracy, the Office of War Information (OWI) in 1942, reintroduced the U.S. government to the propaganda business. Concerned to rebut the propaganda of Goebbels, influential intellectuals like Archibald MacLeish argued the need for democracies to engage in a countervailing crusade in which democratic principles would be promoted with "a strategy of truth."

Since a major concern was to mobilize American public opinion behind the war effort, the OWI had a domestic as well as a foreign arm. Its chief instrument in the battle for men's minds became the radio. Under the leadership of radio journalist Elmer Davis, the OWI's "Voice of America" began to spread the message of democracy throughout the world. It focused on ideological themes like the idealistic war aims proclaimed by FDR and British Prime Minister Winston Churchill in the "Atlantic Charter" in 1941 and the Four Freedoms address in which FDR articulated his vision of a postwar world blessed with freedom of speech and expression, freedom of worship, freedom from want and freedom from fear. According to FDR's confidant, the writer Robert E. Sherwood, "all the U.S. information to the world should be considered as if it were a continuous speech by the President."

In its quest to sell the rest of the world on the virtues of the United States, the OWI spread information on just about every facet of the American way of life. Bad news, whether of wartime strikes or racial disturbances, was often reported in a matter-of-fact way in the style of the widely respected British Broadcasting Corporation. Even though the content might be unflattering, the process of disclosure itself, it was believed, would be perceived positively as an example of the openness of American society. In addition to radio programs featuring newscasts, the OWI printed pamphlets and leaflets and produced documentary films and newsreels. It also set up overseas outposts to report back on local opinion, and it created a system of 28 overseas reading rooms and libraries, expanded after the war to distribute material about the U.S.A.

Although portraying the war as a conflict to defend democracy came easily enough, American wartime diplomacy was notoriously vague: the Administration was preoccupied with military victory to the near exclusion of all else. Given the many disagreements between the allies and the failure to address certain basic issues like the future of Japan and Germany, OWI often found itself long on generalities and short on specifics. Operating in a strategic-policy-planning vacuum, the OWI propaganda program experienced its share of fiascoes, the greatest of all being the fire storm that resulted from its support of General Dwight D. Eisenhower's deal with the pro-fascist Vichy regime in North Africa prior to the November 1942 Allied landings in that region. For those who took democracy seriously, this bargain seemed an unprincipled sellout.

Another problem arose in Italy, where the United States, in apparent disregard of FDR's policy of "unconditional surrender," cut a deal with the post-Mussolini government of Marshal Badoglio, which still retained the odor of fascism. Unfortunately for OWI, which wrongly anticipated that the United States would refuse to do business with

Senator J. William Fulbright (D-Ark.), r., who made a lasting contribution to cultural exchange, served as chairman of the Senate Foreign Relations Committee from 1959 to 1974. He conducted frequent open hearings to help inform the public and spoke out against U.S. military intervention abroad.

Archive Photos

the new regime and its "moronic little king" (as one broadcast described him), its reportage was disavowed by the more pragmatic President.

Less controversial and more successful in war-winning terms were the operations of the militarily controlled Psychological Warfare Branch. PWB dropped leaflets to demoralize the enemy and took over presses and radio stations in conquered cities that it used to herald the arrival of the democratic conquerors. Besides delivering the news, its broadcasts were designed to deceive the Germans about an Allied landing site for the invasion of the Continent. PWB also sought to weaken Japanese morale by hinting at more-lenient surrender terms.

Despite the hopes of many within OWI that its activities would be continued by the State Department after the war, President Harry S. Truman (1945–53) decided on August 31, 1945, to abolish the agency. Though in no immediate danger of disappearing, the cultural programs were in for some tough sledding. An economy-minded Congress was skeptical of cultural expenditures, while State Department officials saw cultural and information affairs as peripheral to the more "manly" stuff of foreign relations.

The remnants of OWI, consisting of some broadcast facilities and overseas libraries, were placed in the State Department alongside the cultural programs, where both hung on tenuously for a few years. In 1947, the House Appropriations Committee deleted funding for the information program.

One of the few bright spots for cultural programs in the immediate postwar years was the creation in 1946 of the Fulbright scholarships. The Fulbright Act, an amendment to the Surplus Property Act of 1944, made available for educational purposes foreign currencies derived from the sale of U.S. assets abroad, such as surplus military supplies. With the proceeds from this ingeniously contrived source of funding, swords were turned into plowshares. Binational foundations were established in many countries to set up procedures for selecting exchange candidates. In the tradition of private cultural control, a Board of Foreign Scholarships was created to make sure that policy was not distorted by short-term political expediency.

The Fulbright program was the exception, however, at a time when the congressional mood was suspicious of foreign policy innovations. Had it not been for the emergence of the cold war, it is likely that the cultural and informational programs would have met an undignified death.

2

The Cold-War Struggle for the Minds of Men

By 1947, distrust of the Soviet Union had led to the adoption of the "containment" policy that committed the United States to an unprecedented degree of global activism and leadership. No doubt the cold war was a political power struggle. However, in a deeper sense, it was an ideological conflict over the relative attractiveness of the belief systems and ways of life of the two main antagonists. In 1946, W. Averell Harriman, then ambassador to Moscow, described the conflict as "a war of ideology and a fight unto the death."

Worried about losing the war of ideas to a sophisticated Communist propaganda apparatus, Congress in January 1948 passed the U.S. Information and Educational Exchange Act. Known as the Smith-Mundt Act after its Senate and House sponsors, this legislation became the basic charter for cultural and informational activities. (The Smith-Mundt Act banned informational activities at home, which suggested congressional wariness of the government's power to distort information for its own purposes.) To pacify those who favored the separation of informational and cultural activities, it provided for the appointment of separate advisory commissions for each function. Throughout all the reorganizations to come, advisory commissions would remain prominent features of the program. They served as private-sector checks upon the government's ability to shape the flow of information and culture.

Within the State Department, which continued to administer cultural exchanges and informational programs, sentiment had shifted strongly in favor of managing these programs for political purposes. Following the failure of private groups to institutionalize exchanges of students, scholars, scientists and library materials between U.S. and Soviet nongovernmental organizations, department officers lost all patience with what they judged to be naive and idealistic assumptions. Instead, they declared cultural and informational activities to be part of "an aggressive program in support of our foreign policy." For these tough realists, these were simply tools for favorably influencing attitudes and opinions within foreign countries.

As the cold war grew more frigid, the nation traveled farther down the road to incorporating information and cultural policy into foreign relations proper. In the Italian elections of 1948, a heavy-handed publicity campaign, whose U.S. funding was an ill-concealed secret, was launched to help prevent a Communist electoral victory. Still, a noisy Soviet "peace offensive" at decade's end, highlighted by a series of peace congresses that attracted cultural luminaries like the artist Pablo Picasso, convinced many that the United States was not doing enough on the cultural front.

Thus was born the rationale for covert financing of groups like the National Student Association and the Congress for Cultural Freedom to do battle with Soviet-front organizations. Funding by the Central Intelligence Agency (CIA) had to be covert because Congress would probably have deemed many of the groups too liberal to merit public support, and open CIA financing would have automatically discredited such groups in the eyes of the rest of the world. Nevertheless, once these arrangements were revealed in the late 1960s, they set off a gale of criticism. However rationalized or defended, the stain of deceitfulness caused by this manipulation of free institutions for propaganda purposes could not easily be washed away.

The creation of certain other ostensibly private but covertly funded organizations raised not so much as a murmur of protest, even in the 1960s. The National Committee for a Free Europe and the American Committee for Liberation from Bolshevism, founded by the CIA in 1949 and 1951 respectively, sought to make political use of emigrés from the U.S.S.R. and its satellite states. These groups in the early 1950s founded Radio Free Europe, which broadcast to Eastern Europe, and Radio Liberty, which targeted the various nationality groups of the Soviet Union. Each of these broadcast news articles, political analyses and reports on international economic and political issues by independent journals. Although their political utility was questionable, they were prime sources of news and enlightenment for dissidents and ordinary citizens whose governments controlled information.

In broadcasting to the Communist-bloc countries, the United States sought to create pathways of communication where the Soviets intended that none exist. A good deal of money and ingenuity was expended to this end. Part of the spending was for sophisticated anti-jamming techniques, including Operation Vagabond, in which a fleet of ships, serving as floating transmitters, continually cruised the Mediterranean to befuddle the Soviet jammers. One of the more bizarre information programs in operation between 1951 and 1956 involved the release of leaflet-filled balloons intended to shower the Iron Curtain countries with news from the West. In 1959, USIA director George Allen, a seasoned diplomat, tried to explain why such activities were being conducted at government expense: "The new diplomacy finds governments aiming directly at the peoples of foreign lands. We do everything we can to reach them, in 35 languages, penetrating their living rooms, bedrooms, cellars, wherever the radio is kept."

Korea and the Escalation of the War of Ideas

Yet another milestone was passed in 1950. When the Korean War broke out in June, it infused the U.S. government with a renewed determination to check the Soviets. In April, President Truman declared a Campaign of Truth as a counter to Soviet propaganda. "There is a terrific struggle going on today to win the minds of the people of the world," he later said. With the inauguration of this information campaign, policy took a significant step away from the "full and fair picture" that had previously been the norm. By this time, because it was widely assumed that "the dissemination of truth is not enough," the information programs were expected to put the highest gloss possible on U.S. foreign policy while scuffing the image of the Soviet bloc.

As an example of the kind of ideological image-making then in fashion, one planning document insisted that the informational or "fast" media ought to be used for *current defensive* propaganda." In 1952, the themes for the year's Strength for Peace With Freedom campaign were (1) "aggression has been stopped"; (2) "the Free World is invincible"; and (3) "the slave system is doomed." In addition to the staple Voice of America broadcasts, a stream of pamphlets and leaflets discussed Korea, the North Atlantic Treaty Organization (NATO), U.S. labor unions, the potency of U.S. military power and the invincibility of the Free World, the progress of the Point Four technical assistance program, the "Power of Youth to Attain Peace Objectives," religion, atomic energy, "slave labor in the Soviet world," a comparison between communism and Nazism, Stalin's slave empire, or "Gulag," and so on. Throughout, American policies were interpreted in the best light possible. Cultural exchanges flourished, too, and not only under the State Department's wing. By 1953, 19 federal agencies were involved in exchanges of persons. Some, as in the case of exchanges of military personnel, were directly related to cold-war policies, whereas scholarly exchanges continued to foster more traditional, apolitical goals.

Given new life by the Korean War, the information program again expanded. Whereas the USIS employed 1,500 persons at its low point in 1948, and spent less than $20 million per year, by 1952 its staff of 8,900 was dispensing more than $100 million annually. At first, the escalation in the war of words reduced communication between the superpowers. In 1952 there was a mutual suspension of the U.S. journal *Amerika,* which was distributed in the U.S.S.R., and its Soviet counterpart in the United States. Contrary to the hopes of many of the pioneers of cultural exchanges, the cold war was not being thawed by dialogue.

The Eisenhower Years

With the election of Eisenhower to the presidency in 1952, the informational and cultural programs became full-fledged weapons in the nation's cold-war diplomatic arsenal. Eisenhower believed strongly in cultural exchanges, but he was an even more zealous exponent of using information and psychological warfare in the struggle against the Soviets. Prior to his electoral triumph, Eisenhower spoke privately of "the very urgent necessity for *skillful* propaganda on the part of the allies, of the highest quality and of adequate volume," adding that "if it is really skillful, its governmental source, support and connection will be carefully concealed."

As a budgetary conservative, Eisenhower believed that an emphasis on military means alone threatened to bankrupt the United States. As a recent convert to the idea that superpower conflicts were not resolvable by war in the modern era, he was convinced that other means needed to be explored. Since the cold war was a struggle between coalitions, the ability to foment dissension became a potentially decisive way for each side to erode the enemy's will and staying power.

Eisenhower therefore decided to preside over a full-blown reorganization of the informational and cultural apparatus in 1953. In the last year of Truman's term, both informational and cultural activities had enjoyed semiautonomous status within the Department of State. Eisenhower oversaw the creation of the USIA, a separate administrative entity, whose primary purpose was "to persuade foreign peoples that it lies in their own interest to take actions which are consistent with the national objectives of the United States."

In deference to the sensibilities of the educational establishment and its guardian angel, Senator J. William Fulbright (D–Ark.), the State Department retained policy control over cultural exchanges. In the field, however, a single public affairs officer, or PAO, taking orders from USIA, was responsible for oversight of both cultural and informational policy. Administratively, the cultural affairs officers, or CAO's, were wholly creatures of the "infocrats."

In practice, much depended on the quality of the personnel in the field. In the case of PAO's who were sensitive to the danger of politicizing their tasks, their relationship to the cultural attachés often amounted to a cordial division of labor. The PAO would deal with the media, the ministries, the political parties and the business contacts, whereas the CAO would cultivate educators, artists, intellectuals and the like. But there was no doubt where administrative power lay. The information bureaucracy controlled assignments and transfers, budgets, staffs and promotions. The higher rungs of the career ladder within USIA were occupied by those who viewed both functions in national-interest terms. Over a period of 40 years, this splayed system would become institutionalized in more than 200 USIS posts overseas.

McCarthyism

In the 1950s, cold-war domestic pressures also compromised the ideal of a free and open exchange of ideas. While the agency prospered in terms of budgets and manpower, USIA morale plummeted under the onslaught of the junior Republican senator from Wisconsin, Joseph R. McCarthy. Convinced that traitors existed within USIA's ranks, McCarthy launched a campaign against the agency. In short order, his investigators reported unearthing at least 75 different titles by "Communist authors" in USIS libraries. In a letter to John Foster Dulles dated April 7, 1953, McCarthy asked the secretary of state why "none of the Acheson-Truman team have come forward to explain how they thought they were fighting communism by purchasing, distributing, and placing the U.S. stamp of approval on a vast number of well-known Communist authors."

Novels by Howard Fast, a leftist author, and a biography of the left-wing Negro actor and singer Paul Robeson were hastily yanked from the shelves. But that was only the beginning. By mid-1953, over 300 titles by 144 authors had been purged from USIS libraries by frantic librarians who had to guess what McCarthy had in mind. The panic generated by McCarthy's inquisition led to more than a few totally inadvertent injustices, as harried officials failed to distinguish between Ring Lardner and Ring Lardner Jr. or between Bernard Berenson and Bernard Berelson.

Even though the number of people—in USIA and elsewhere—directly affected by McCarthyism was small by comparison with political purges in other countries, the damage done was considerable. Ca-

Archive Photos

Senator Joseph R. McCarthy (R-Wisc.), who in February 1950 won national attention by charging the State Department had been infiltrated by Communists, testifying before a Senate committee. In 1953 he launched a campaign against USIA.

reers and lives were ruined, while the agency's concern to maintain its anti-Communist credentials, even at the expense of the principle of freedom of ideas, was institutionally devastating. USIA soon found it difficult to recruit competent personnel. The Voice of America suffered particularly severe damage from the senator's broadsides. More important from the foreign policy standpoint, McCarthyism did grave damage to the image of the United States as an open society that the government was trying so hard to project abroad.

The Cold War and Educational Exchanges with the U.S.S.R.

McCarthyism was harmful, but not fatal, thanks in large measure to the President's persistence. Eisenhower, George Allen recalled, "believed devotedly, almost mystically, in the value of people-to-people contacts." At the Geneva summit of 1955, best known for his open-skies proposal for mutual photographic surveillance,

Eisenhower pushed hard for a program of educational exchanges. Although Congress in 1956 provided funds for cultural activities abroad, Eisenhower was perennially dissatisfied with the limited scope of the American effort.

Eisenhower resented the depiction of the United States as "a race of materialists, whose only diversions are golf, football, horse racing, and an especially brutalized brand of boxing. Our successes are described in terms of automobiles and not in terms of worthwhile cultural works of any kind. Spiritual and intellectual values are deemed to be almost nonexistent in our country." This stereotyped image of the nation cried out for an official remedy that cultural exchanges seemed well-equipped to provide.

For Eisenhower, the underlying source of cold-war disagreement was lack of contact. "The Soviets fear strangers," he claimed, "both because of what they will learn and what the Russian people will learn from them." In a moment of frustration, he drafted a letter to Soviet leader Nikita S. Khrushchev in February 1956. Because young people seemed more willing and able than elderly cold warriors to "absorb new ideas, new thoughts, new information, as compared to the difficulty that their elders experience," Ike proposed what he called "a great experiment"—inviting a few thousand Soviet students for a year's stay in the United States as guests, with all expenses paid. "Nothing of our ways or purposes would be concealed," he promised. This would be "not an exchange but an unconditional invitation." If accepted, "we would repudiate the fate of youth as victims of prejudice and misunderstanding."

Dulles Skeptical about Exchanges

This letter never left Washington. As his personal secretary recalled, "he was never quite able to sell the State Department." His secretary of state, Dulles, while agreed in principle on the desirability of exchanges, "regarded President Eisenhower as rather naive in thinking that this kind of thing was really going to make much change in the world." Always afraid of creating an impression of weakness, Dulles was particularly concerned that exchanges might produce a relaxation of alliance solidarity and a softening of the will to resist the Soviets.

Whenever Ike sought to resurrect his proposals, Dulles would note, quite correctly, that the program was hardly as innocent and well-meaning as the President made it appear. As Dulles put it, "the purpose of student exchange is not merely to import understanding but to subvert the Soviet form of government."

Some internal obstacles to increased communication were raised in debates within the National Security Council (NSC) on the question of negotiating a treaty on cultural exchanges with the Soviets. In March 1955 the NSC was concerned with "countering foreign talk that it is the United States, rather than the U.S.S.R., that is maintaining an 'iron curtain.' " Though the United States was obviously the far more open society, there was in fact more than a grain of truth to such accusations. The U.S. Postal Service was avidly intercepting subversive literature and preventing its distribution. Out of fear of commercial and technological spying, visitors from the Eastern bloc were admitted only rarely, by discretionary authority of the attorney general, under the terms of the restrictive Immigration and Nationality Act of 1952. The act's fingerprinting requirements led to embarrassing complaints about visitors from all over the world being subjected to police-state surveillance.

Although an NSC document admitted that "this situation is causing damage, and may cause further damage, to the U.S. prestige and the U.S. reputation for liberal world leadership," a liberalization of policy carried many apparent disadvantages. There were fears of commercial, technological and political espionage, of propaganda exploitation, and of being dazzled by the bravura performances of hand-picked Soviet visitors. The result, complained Secretary of State Dulles, was that exchanges were "hopelessly bogged down."

Gradually, policy began to turn around. Strategic logic, said a State Department paper of June 1956, argued on behalf of the United States taking the lead in ending the cultural freeze. "Our foreign policies are necessarily *defensive*, so far as the use of force is concerned," it said, "but they can be *offensive* in terms of promoting a desire for greater freedom." Therefore, "East-West exchanges should be an implementation of a positive U.S. foreign policy." Despite fears of sending the wrong signal to allies by fraternizing with the enemy, the debate was ended when Dulles insisted that "nothing catastrophic was going to happen as a result of the adoption of this new policy." While Eisenhower agreed that unmonitored exchanges were "a serious danger," it was decided that appropriate safeguards could always be put in place.

Because all existing exchanges had been discontinued in the wake of the Soviet crushing of the Hungarian revolt in October 1956, negotiations with the Soviets did not get under way until the following year. By that time, private groups were beginning to express impatience with the government, and newspaper criticisms about hidebound policy were starting to appear. Public opinion polls and newspapers solidly favored the resumption of exchanges. Bilateral talks began in October on a small-scale program, and Congress obliged by waiving most fingerprinting requirements for stays of less than 12 months.

On January 27, 1958, the two countries finally signed a cultural agreement. The program was limited to exchanges of scholars, students and relatively innocuous tours of performing artists, generally under conditions of strict reciprocity. On occasion, exhibits were permitted, the most famous of these being the model American kitchen in Moscow where Vice President Richard M. Nixon engaged Khrushchev in vigorous debate over the relative merits of their two social systems. Overall, the agreement was too modest in scope to be anything more than symbolic. Yet the permitted contacts at least held out the hope that the two nations were capable of using words, as well as power, to communicate.

Promoting Free-World Solidarity

Notwithstanding the many attempts to penetrate the Soviet bloc, in the 1950s the free-world front was by far the more important theater of ideological battle. An advisory committee in 1953 suggested that fewer resources be devoted to broadcasting to the U.S.S.R. because it was "difficult to envisage any positive results which could now be achieved by provocative propaganda." The emphasis was more on maintaining free-world solidarity than on breaking Soviet morale. "We are in competition with Soviet communism primarily for the opinion of the free world," said one document. "We are (especially) concerned with the uncommitted, the wavering, the confused, the apathetic, or the doubtful within the free world." In Western Europe and other areas, the interest was in getting at leaders who in turn could reach mass audiences beyond the reach of the USIA.

Eisenhower also tried to stimulate the creation of a "people-to-people program" in which private individuals and organizations took the initiative in promoting exchanges of all kinds. Businessmen provided foreign speakers, held conventions abroad, and created foreign affiliates, while civic groups of every variety exchanged people and took up book collections. At first, Ike was "quite astonished" at the rapid growth of the program. However, this initiative petered out as private sources of funding, particularly from the philanthropic foundations, remained untapped for fear that newcomers would "barge into this field and take over everything that everybody else has been doing." There was a reluctance, too, in the philanthropic community to be used as a cat's paw of the government in the cultural field. Of more than 40 committees originally organized, by 1957, only half were still active. The following year, the director of the program reported abjectly that "we have been extremely unsuccessful in raising funds for the people-to-people program to date." By then, the program was in a state of terminal atrophy, even if it persists to this day.

Having defined the cold war as a battle for the minds of men, by 1958 Eisenhower remarked despondently that "our public relations problem almost defies solution." The following year, a survey entitled "As Others See Us: The United States Through Foreign Eyes" presented an unflattering assessment of the American image abroad. Still, given the need to preserve allies and prevent neutrals from sliding into the enemy camp, the courting of world opinion remained a major factor in the foreign policy of the cold war.

Cold-War Decline

Elected in 1960, President John F. Kennedy (JFK) was strikingly sensitive to the capacity of ideas and images to influence the world balance of power. In his campaign speeches, Kennedy had fretted repeatedly about the ominous trend of world opinion, the image of America in decline, and the willingness of many observers in Third World nations to place their bets on the Communist side as likely victors in the cold war. During his presidency, relations with the Soviet

Union came alarmingly near the point of war on a number of occasions. However, after bringing cold-war tensions to their stormiest level, the Kennedy Administration also ushered in the first soft breezes of détente. These contradictory tendencies were reflected in the ups and downs of the cultural and informational programs during the 1960s.

The Soviets dramatically expanded the scope of their cultural efforts by establishing a People's Friendship University in Moscow in 1960. By 1962, enrollment in the Soviet Union included some 4,000 state-supported students from the Third World. Meanwhile, the U.S. government funded scholarships for fewer then 3,000 foreign students, a small proportion of the 48,000 then studying in the United States. For many of the foreign students in America, life was very difficult. Poor language skills and little or no orientation beforehand meant they were often thrown upon their meager personal resources. Little in the way of institutional support existed to assure their ability to devote sufficient time to their studies.

A swelling chorus argued that the United States was falling behind in the struggle to win over the minds of men. According to Arthur M. Schlesinger Jr., JFK "had the feeling that under the Eisenhower Administration the United States looked to the world like a business-dominated country, and he wanted to put the intellectual foot forward." In a meeting with the Board of Foreign Scholarships and the U.S. Advisory Commission on Educational Exchange, Kennedy argued:

There is no better way of helping the new nations of Latin America, Africa and Asia in their present pursuit of freedom and better living conditions than by assisting them to develop their human resources through education. Likewise there is no better way to strengthen our bond of understanding and friendship with older nations than through educational and cultural interchange.

The status of cultural programs was thus upgraded in 1961 by two separate developments. First, the Fulbright-Hays Act consolidated various educational and exchange programs in the interest of promoting "international understanding" and provided increased dollar funding for expanded exchanges. Then, seeking to enhance the prestige of cultural diplomacy and provide some centralized direction for the existing mélange of programs, Kennedy created a new position within the State Department, an assistant secretary of state for educational and cultural affairs. The first appointee to fill this post (CU, for culture, in State Department shorthand) was Philip H. Coombs, previously an executive of the Ford Foundation's Fund for the Advancement of Education.

During the Kennedy years, the design and focus of the informational and cultural programs in foreign countries also changed. With a view to tailoring discrete messages to specific audiences, the USIA in Washington asked posts annually to formulate themes and to identify the audience to be reached; this was then translated into a "country plan." Kennedy also added an advisory function to USIA's mission, but the agency has never broken into the big league of foreign policy formulation. This basic scheme remains in effect today, though it was revised in 1978 to take into account "communications tensions," listed and reported on annually by field officers, between the United States and other nations. These might include anything from culturally rooted misunderstandings to opposing political perspectives.

Although CU was supposedly given the mandate to coordinate the cultural affairs programs and exchanges, there was no clear conception of how this was to be done. Coombs spent a good deal of time in supervising task forces and trying to generate new ideas, but the job carried little executive authority. Understandably, he complained in frustration about "driving without a license." When his mentor, Under Secretary of State Chester Bowles, lost the confidence of the President and left the State Department, Coombs found himself administratively helpless against more seasoned bureaucrats with established power bases.

Coombs had more than his share of difficulties with USIA, which played political hardball with more power and finesse than he was able to muster. Its new director, Edward R. Murrow, a cult figure in broadcasting circles, was determined to put his agency on the bureaucratic map. Thanks to his charisma, Murrow raised the prestige of the information function and reasserted its primacy. Meanwhile, other agencies resisted having their exchange programs "coordinated" by the State Department. Added to Coombs' headaches was the disastrous publicity arising from the tour of comedian and entertainer Joey

Adams, which was portrayed as a taxpayer-supported junket undertaken for the amusement of foreign heads of state.

CU, meanwhile, suffered annual tortures at the hands of the House Appropriations subcommittee, chaired by the skeptical John Rooney (D-N.Y.). For example, the CU budget request for exchanges and "cultural presentations" in the performing arts for fiscal year (FY) 1962 was slashed from $65 million to $40 million. Culture was a tough sell to Congress, whereas information could more easily be tailored to macho cold-war rationales. Given all the difficulties, Coombs lasted little more than one year before resigning his position in frustration.

However much American statesmen liked to depict the cold war as a struggle for world opinion, for the cultural programs the rhetoric of commitment during the Kennedy years far exceeded the meager budgetary realities. Because the traditional national-security apparatus seemed far better suited to dealing with vital issues of credibility and morale, money and attention continued to flow in its direction.

In the early 1960s, the Vietnam War brought further changes in the conduct of cold-war foreign policy. For one thing, the USIA became heavily involved in trying to win international approval of American intervention in Southeast Asia, a campaign that found few subscribers among either friends or foes. The agency could do little to hold back a global tide of criticism that rose ominously in response to each American escalation. Beyond that, the Vietnam debacle also cast doubt upon the political premises of the information programs.

Although President Lyndon B. Johnson (1963–69) at first promised to expand American efforts in international education, skyrocketing military budgets meant that his Administration came nowhere near fulfilling his promises. From a high point of $61 million for FY 1963, the CU budget dropped by almost 50 percent to $31 million by 1969.

Administratively, things went from bad to worse. CU became a bureaucratic revolving door, with 11 assistant secretaries holding office over the next 17 years. When presidential appointees did stick around long enough to learn about CU, they were disappointed with what they found.

Still more changes took place in the 1970s. In the atmosphere of muckraking and distrust of government that pervaded the decade of the Watergate political scandal, revelations emerged concerning secret funding practices. The new emphasis on openness led in 1973 to Radio Free Europe and Radio Liberty coming in out of the cold; Congress created a Board for International Broadcasting that enabled these two organs to continue transmitting to Eastern Europe and the U.S.S.R. without CIA funding. In response to growing criticism that the system of divided responsibility between the Department of State and USIA was not working, yet another sweeping organizational change was set in motion.

Reorganization a Blow to Cultural Programs

In 1975, the year that Fulbright left the Senate, Dr. Frank Stanton of CBS News was appointed to chair an independent, privately funded review of U.S. cultural and informational programs. The Stanton report suggested the creation of a new and autonomous agency. Despite Fulbright's plea against CU being "swallowed up in a huge operation where it would be absorbed into the large mass," the reorganization-minded Administration of President Jimmy Carter (1977–81) created the U.S. International Communication Agency (USICA). Only Radio Free Europe and Radio Liberty remained as separate governmental organizations under a board of governors. The Voice of America, meanwhile, was given quasi-independent status after 1978. An advisory commission on "public diplomacy," the new (and ill-defined) term, replaced the two separate commissions on culture and information.

This "fundamental" reform, like all its predecessors, proved a mere rearrangement of the bureaucratic furniture, and an unsatisfactory one at that. For supporters of educational exchange, the coming of "public diplomacy" had all the earmarks of a hostile takeover that made information king. The change was especially traumatic for former CU staffers who were forced to move from their neat State Department offices into dingy accommodations in USIA headquarters. CU's autonomy had already been significantly eroded when it was induced to join hands with USIA in 1971 in producing a joint country plan. As Richard Arndt, a 24-year veteran of CU and USIA, put it, "the goal became the same: 'influentials' and 'leaders' were to be 'reached,' then quantified as 'exposures.' "

During the presidency of Ronald Reagan (1981–89), as active combat against the Soviet "evil empire" once again became an obsession, public diplomacy was expected to do its part. Indeed, it was one-sidedly redefined as "those actions of the government designed to generate support for our national-security objectives." The new emphasis was on selling the American point of view. The 1978 reorganization's commendable "second mandate," which charged the agency with interpreting the rest of the world to the United States, was lost in the shuffle. The effects on morale were serious and the number of educational and cultural specialists working in the agency began to decline. As one observer remarked, under Reagan the USIA's "output was at times propagandistic and simplistic."

Political pressures on the cultural programs came from outside the agency, too. Congress in the 1980s began increasingly to earmark exchange moneys for pet projects that fitted the ideological enthusiasm of the moment. Following the collapse of the U.S.S.R., fellowships were earmarked for formerly Communist countries with the idea of aiding their transition to democracy. However laudable this goal, congressional micromanagement took the policymaking function from the hands of the agency and restricted the availability of funds for other, perhaps more worthy, purposes.

Public Diplomacy Stages a Comeback

For all that, public diplomacy received a second wind in the 1980s. One of the first steps in the revival was to reclaim the old USIA name, since USICA was too easily confused with CIA. Budgetarily, too, the USIA managed to more than hold its own, thanks to the personal friendship of director Charles Z. Wick (1981–89) with President Reagan. New information programs dedicated to achieving cold-war objectives were readily approved and new initiatives were launched. Radio Martí was aimed specifically at Cuban audiences to, as the President said, "break Fidel Castro's monopoly on news and information within Cuba." One of Wick's pet projects was the establishment of a satellite TV system called Worldnet, which made possible long-distance interviews and teleconferences between USIS centers and individuals in studios in the United States.

After threatening to cut severely the educational-exchange programs, Wick backed off in the face of an unexpected outcry from an

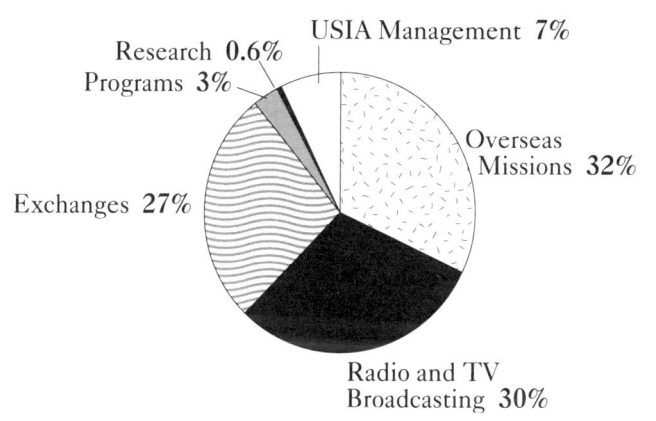

USIA's 1993 Operating Expenses by Major Activity*

- USIA Management 7%
- Research 0.6%
- Programs 3%
- Overseas Missions 32%
- Exchanges 27%
- Radio and TV Broadcasting 30%

*Excludes VOA construction, Office of the Inspector General and grants to the National Endowment for Democracy, East-West Center and North-South Center.

outraged community of Fulbright supporters. In the end, Congress doubled its appropriation for the agency. While much of the money flowed into informational coves like visitors' programs, educational exchanges also managed to profit significantly from this ideologically inspired surge of largesse. At the same time, Congress sought to assure that exchanges were "fenced off" from the agency's information programs.

This "second cold war" was unexpectedly brief. By 1991, when the Soviet Union collapsed and was swept into the dustbin of history, it seemed to many that the rationale for public diplomacy had disappeared. To such critics, the cultural and informational programs ought to be honorably discharged, demobilized, and their functions turned over, without funding, to the private sector. As part of a larger rethinking of the purposes of government taking place in the mid-1990s, arguments on behalf of retaining these functions were greeted with growing skepticism.

By this time, both the informational and cultural sides of public diplomacy were in deep difficulty, victims of huge budget deficits spawned in the 1980s. It was hard at times to see the difference between reinventing government and disinventing it. The Clinton Administration quickly phased out the Munich stations of Radio Free Europe and Radio Liberty, reduced staff from 1,600 to 400, and consolidated these broadcast operations in a new bureau in USIA following a noisy bureaucratic squabble. Radio and TV Martí were threatened, though finally included in the first Clinton budget. However, many USIA services were discontinued, among them exhibitions, magazines, book fairs and book exchanges. Whereas USIA had employed 13,000 people in 1967, by 1994 the number had dropped to about 9,000. Even the flagship of the cultural programs, the Fulbright scholarships, seemed in danger of being mothballed. One worried observer noted that "insiders and close observers of the Fulbright program today wonder if it can survive into the next century."

Policymakers within USIA argued that in the post-cold-war world the need for public diplomacy was greater than ever. Given the greater international role played by public opinion, the shift in emphasis from military to economic and other "soft" issues, and the growing need for collective action, they claimed that the agency could "make an even greater contribution to furthering U.S. interests in the world than it has in the past." The legitimate concern for economy could be met through downsizing, reorganization and other efficiencies. More bang for the buck could be delivered by relying on electronic information. These and other measures could "yield a higher quality and more timely product."

Nevertheless, at the beginning of 1996, the agency's future was very much in suspense. In March 1995, the new chairman of the Senate Foreign Relations Committee, Jesse A. Helms (R–N.C.), called the USIA part of "a constellation of money-absorbing, incoherent satellites." Only radical organizational measures, he insisted, would get rid of this "complete mess." Following Helms's suggestions, in June 1995 the House voted to eliminate the agency and absorb its operations into the Department of State, with the expectation that the

Senate would shortly follow suit. But the budget-cutters had more in mind than simply giving the agency's operations a new home. As *The New York Times* reported, congressional subcommittees were "seeking to cut off financing of its main activities: broadcasting and educational exchanges." "There are higher priorities for spending our money," said Brent Scowcroft, President Bush's national security adviser.

As ever, the agency's most difficult job of selling lay in convincing the American people of its right to exist. The primary concern on Capitol Hill was economy, and it was not clear that many members of Congress knew much about the policy issues involved or cared to know. For the cultural community, the prospects were for continued programmatic confusion and funding cutbacks. Despite an unhappy coexistence within USIA, the likelihood was that life within the State Department, with reduced funding, would be even less hospitable to cultural exchange.

3

Conflicts and Conundrums

To MANY of their defenders, the need for cultural and informational programs is self-evident. According to J.M. Mitchell, the author of one of the few works on cultural diplomacy, "there is a ready-made rationale in favor of cultural relations" because people accept diplomacy, and if they can be persuaded that culture and information contribute to the effectiveness of diplomacy, "then they can accept that, too." The breadth and complexity of foreign relations in the twentieth century would seem to call for the employment of all available diplomatic instruments. The fact that many nations find utility in public diplomacy suggests that it has become a standard implement of the diplomatic tool kit.

Most Americans have yet to be convinced. In a country where an internationalist foreign policy has been accepted only with reluctance, and where a populist anti-intellectualism has more than once roused the political furies, the relationship of informational and cultural programs to national security has often seemed obscure. As a result, in the course of a relatively brief history, American cultural and informational programs have experienced more than their share of political difficulties.

These problems have permeated every dimension of foreign policy. Starting from the ground floor in the public-private relationship, there has long been uncertainty over the legitimacy of these two activities as elements of a liberal foreign policy. Aside from the question of whether they belong in foreign policy at all, the issue of how and to what degree they ought to be used by government has been a source of continuous vexation. And however problematic their relationship to the larger diplomatic community and their role in policy, their governmental role has been complicated by chronic tension between champions of either cultural exchange or information. Lastly, when one looks at the international implications of these activities and asks about their effectiveness, it is apparent that the promotion of cultural interaction and the encouragement of the free flow of ideas are extremely questionable activities.

Do cultural and informational activities belong in foreign policy? Other nations think so. On a per capita basis, many countries, including France and Spain, spend much more on public diplomacy than the United States. Taiwan and Japan also have official cultural programs. Germany has foundations formed by political parties, like the Friedrich Ebert Stiftung, that provide informal support for exchanges and intellectual activities. The British Council conducts some exemplary cultural programs. Whatever the propagandist connotations of cultural and informational programs may have been earlier in this century, the tendency today is to conduct them in smooth, professional and noncontroversial fashion.

The United States has never been able to articulate a satisfactory *permanent* rationale. The chief barrier to successful institutionalization has been the limited role allotted to the government by the two branches of liberalism that dominate American political thought. Because culture and information are domains that belong naturally to the private sector and to the states in the U.S. federal system, Americans tend to be sensitive about government intrusion in these spheres, be it for domestic or foreign purposes. Education was exclusively local and private until the 1950s, and the First Amendment, by creating a press establishment jealous of its autonomy, continues to limit the government's ability to impose its views upon journalists. Following the pattern of intervention for emergency wartime reasons, the federal government injected itself into the realm of education only as a consequence of cold-war dissatisfaction or, as in the case of the 1944 GI Bill of Rights, to prevent massive postwar unemployment. It is not at all surprising, then, that one also hears calls today for abolishing the Department of Education now that the cold-war emergency has passed.

Controversy over Cultural Activities

Just as important a limiting factor as fear of governmental control of culture, education, the press and ideas has been populist resentment, often anti-elitist and nativist in thrust. The experience of the National Endowment for the Humanities and the National Endowment for the Arts, whose grants have often occasioned howls of disbelief from an offended public, suggests that culture is freighted with potential for controversy. A few examples of the pitfalls of cultural policy should be enough to make the point.

One particularly disastrous episode took place in 1947 when the State Department put together a traveling exhibit of abstract American paintings, called "Advancing American Art," in an attempt to demonstrate to foreign audiences that the United States was indeed a land of "high culture," i.e., a nation capable of supporting artistic and intellectual activities of the most advanced kind. Although enormously successful overseas, the exhibit turned into a political fiasco at home when congressional conservatives singled out paintings that no one seemed able to understand as examples of wasteful government spending. At an uproarious House Appropriations Committee hearing, Assistant Secretary of State William Benton was challenged, with ill-concealed glee, to describe from point-blank visual range the content of the more nonrepresentational works that were included in the collection.

This was bad enough. But once it was revealed that a few of the artists had radical inclinations, conservatives began to argue, in all seriousness, that the paintings were culturally subversive. Radicalism in art, they insisted, threatened to undermine all traditional norms and values. Modern art (no less odious to the Soviet Union's cultural commissars) was therefore profoundly un-American. Thus identified with leftist radicalism, cultural internationalism became a symbol of an encroaching modernity that was threatening to subvert the American way of life.

Another cultural uproar was sparked by an exhibit entitled "Sport in Art," assembled by the American Federation of Art for *Sports Illustrated*. This collection was supposed to tour the United States before being sent to Australia by the USIA for the 1956 Olympics in Melbourne. Anti-Communist groups in Dallas, Texas, began to demand the withdrawal of certain paintings in the exhibit because of the alleged pro-Communist sympathies of the artists. As the tumult built, USIA director Theodore C. Streibert (1953–56) pulled the plug not only on the Olympic display but on a number of other exhibits as well. Even an overseas tour of Arturo Toscanini's NBC symphony was canceled because of the alleged pro-Communist views of a small number of its musicians.

Alleged radicalism has not been the only problem. The cultural programs have also been vulnerable because of their elitism and cosmopolitanism. On more than one occasion, Congress and the public have had great difficulty in understanding the relevance of grants made for esoteric intellectual purposes with only a tenuous connection to foreign policy. The fundamental concept of two-way exchange has also alarmed those who feared the influx of strange and subversive foreign ideas. Congress has been persuaded to open its purse strings in times of crisis, but in the best of times the programs have had to fight a powerful undertow of suspicion about their democratic and ideological bona fides.

U.S. Educational System a Magnet

While the existence of America's impressive mass-media apparatus has often been used as an argument against the informational programs, the same type of criticism could be applied to the educational-exchange programs. These have seemed unnecessary to some because of the global reach of America's educational system. Attracted by a peerless system of higher education, in 1978, 31 percent of all foreign students in the world were studying in the United States, more than twice the percentage of the next highest country, France.

In absolute terms, in 1983, there were some 325,000 foreign students in the United States, two thirds at the undergraduate level; with the passage of a decade, that number would swell to 438,000. Of this group, only 2 percent were supported by the U.S. government. Just as significant, by the early 1990s, about 72,000 American students, a record number, were studying abroad. Given this trend toward international education, there was increasing talk among administrators of forming new "global universities." Government, it seems, had little to do with this educational gold rush. Indeed, one study concluded that all this had been accomplished with "no national policy concerning foreign students."

Even in areas where exchanges had been restricted during the cold war, the private sector had performed well by placing its programs in mothballs and biding its time until the day when private exchanges could once again be resumed in large numbers. The most dramatic case was China, a country that released a wave of eager students to American graduate schools in the late 1970s in the aftermath of the adoption of the Four Modernizations program of Deng Xiaoping. This explosion of interchange among recent ideological enemies was eloquent testimony to the lasting influence of the pioneering cultural efforts made earlier in the twentieth century.

Now that the cold war is over, it might seem as if the time is ripe to eliminate the cultural and informational programs. The 1990s, in some ways, resemble the 1920s, a decade in which Americans believed that with the vanquishing of autocracy during World War I it was time to allow the "natural" private forces of commerce and culture to do their work unobstructed by politics. Even some past supporters no longer see the need for governmental intrusiveness, whereas others question the continuing outlay of scarce tax money for functions that the private sector seems to be handling quite well. Arguments for retaining these activities are met with skepticism as examples of the tendency of bureaucracies to perpetuate themselves by contriving new missions.

Bureaucratic Problems

Public diplomacy has also lacked prestige in a foreign policy bureaucracy dominated by professionals still accustomed to thinking about international relations in "hard" terms of power. Far from atypical was the Foreign Service Officer who asked: "Do you really believe in this public diplomacy stuff?" For most foreign policy professionals, glamour, achievement and recognition are to be found in the traditional careers. The cultural programs were held in such low esteem by careerists that, in the 1960s, Coombs complained they were "the underprivileged children living in the slum area of U.S. foreign policy." Coombs was not far off the mark, for CU had long been used as a dumping ground by the State Department for burned-out Foreign Service Officers who were no longer deemed capable of filling more demanding positions.

The problem of finding a legitimate mission has been aggravated by the liberal aversion to propaganda. The early cultural program went to considerable lengths to insulate itself from political direction by the government. The information program, although eager as ever to make a contribution to foreign policy, has always felt the need to pass a "white glove" test on the truthfulness of the information it was purveying. The result was a built-in contradiction: politics and deceit, which operated in the impure environment of the real world, always threatened to contaminate activities that needed ideally to take place in a clean room.

The occasional revelations of CIA involvement, whether in the secret funding in the 1950s and 1960s of radio broadcasting or the subsidizing of cultural groups like the Congress for Cultural Freedom and the National Student Association, seemed to many to underscore the need to separate these activities from the government. The propagandist temptation to subsidize, and perhaps manipulate, private groups that traded in intellectual freedom was used as a prime example of the conceptual incompatibility of culture and power. Thus, the never-ending reorganizations of the cultural and informational programs seemed vain attempts to settle administratively a problem that could not be resolved philosophically. A term like "public diplomacy"—officially adopted in the 1970s—was a euphemism that merely papered over the predicament.

And if all these problems were not enough, the partisans of information and culture have at times gone at one another with such vehemence that it would be pardonable to conclude that they, rather than the Soviets, were the enemy. It was during the early post-World War II years that the philosophical breach between information and culture emerged. Locked bureaucratically into an unhappy marriage within the State Department, the two sides began a struggle for definition and recognition that has continued, off and on, to the present day.

Advocates of cultural exchange have tended to represent their activity as uncorrupted. The political payoff, if any, would come sometime in the future as a result of improved international understanding as cultural differences narrowed. By contrast, detractors have all too easily written off cultural exchange as otherworldly naïveté. For informational types searching for a legitimating mission, their activities have seemed better-suited to supporting specific foreign policy goals with a visible payoff. This political orientation has given them the appearance, in the eyes of cultural advocates, of propagandists at worst or, at best, slick purveyors of misleading messages.

Yet another series of problems has tended to revolve around the effects of these programs. Is informational diplomacy essential to national security, as many advocates have asserted? Unfortunately, there is no socioscientific way of measuring its efficacy. The cultural programs are also inherently resistant to quantification. Even so, it does not take very much insight to argue that neither has been crucial to the short-term success of foreign policy.

Cultural Diplomacy and the Cold War

One way of approaching the issue would be to ask whether victory in the cold war was achieved by cultural or informational means. Was it a triumph of ideas over power? The great Soviet writer Alexander Solzhenitsyn, for example, has praised the U.S. radio broadcasts for continuing to provide dissidents with access to the truths that the Soviet regime was determined to suppress. While it would be tempting for advocates of public diplomacy to claim credit, they have scant reason to do so. The end of communism was the result of disillusionment within certain segments of the Soviet elite whose ideological convictions were corroded by the growing understanding that communism was a failure as a system for satisfying human wants.

The Russian people and the Soviet nationality groups, by contrast, seemed relatively little affected, except perhaps by their lust for the products available in the West's consumer utopia. But their envy and acquisitiveness were not matched by an understanding or acceptance of the psychological and cultural characteristics so indispensable to the success of Western capitalist society. In the case of the former East Germany, exposure to the Federal Republic of Germany's television over the course of 20 years produced dissatisfaction with the standard of living, but collapse came only after a loss of will among Communist leaders no longer keen on using brute force to maintain discipline among their subjects.

It is also doubtful whether the cultural and informational programs can take credit for maintaining a favorable climate of opinion in the non-Communist world. To a significant extent, the developed West was bound together by common civilizational values that had long been in the making. It is unlikely that informational salesmanship or cultural exchanges alone would have been successful had not America's allies perceived them as being consistent with commonly held values.

Cultural Backlash

It is also possible to argue that for all the persons favorably influenced, there have been individuals repelled by what they saw in the United States. Exposure to Western ideas and values does not necessarily result in dialogue and mutual understanding. That cultural relations could have a backlash was evident from the situation in Iran. Iran had nearly 50,000 students studying in the United States at the time of the fundamentalist revolution in 1979. The presence within Iran of an increasingly secular, Westernized elite clearly contributed to the explosion of fundamentalist resentment.

Informational programs at least aspire to political status, but the cultural programs, which have never made claims to political potency, labor under an additional burden: the intuitive belief of many realists that they are trivial. This objection can be easily fended off, but to do so requires a rejection of the stereotyped image of cultural relations. Cultural exchanges are associated with a well-meaning innocence that seems out of place in the adult world of power. They have an air of do-goodism about them. They represent a trusting internationalism of the "to know you is to get to like you" variety, a high-brow version of the sentimentality evident in TV commercials that exhort viewers to "reach out and touch someone" or claim "the world is a whole lot better when the people of the world all get together."

The accusation that cultural relations are a visionary activity is quite accurate, but the desire to break down cultural barriers is hardly innocuous or innocent. Whatever their actual impact, it is difficult to imagine a foreign policy activity that is more serious, even subversive, in intent. The point comes across more clearly if one suggests that they have been misnamed. They might, more precisely, have been called *anticultural* relations. That is because, at bottom, they are about deracination, the uprooting of traditional cultural identities. Liberalism assumes that customary beliefs, which are based on local traditions, prevent peoples from communicating on the basis of a human nature that they have in common. Because cultural exchange promotes change, and change is painful and problematic, it often entails a renunciation of traditional values. At the practical level, this problem becomes visible in the so-called brain drain, in which many Western-educated intellectuals have abandoned their native lands to pursue a more attractive life in the West.

Viewed from this perspective, the problem in cultural relations is nothing less than culture itself. Anthropology, with its sensitivity to the centrality of culture and the importance of symbolism in human affairs, suggests that culture *is* the basis of understanding, that our humanity can only be expressed through culture. If this is so, cultural internationalists are asking people to reconsider who and what they are, to cast their identities into doubt, and to question their traditional values without knowing what lies in store for them at the end of this painful process of transformation. From the perspective of those who are being asked to change, then, it is easy to see how the systematic pursuit of deracination could appear as a form of dehumanization or, at best, as a cultural imperialism in which a new identity is being rammed down the throats of the weak. Far from being trivial and harmless, then, for many people the effects of "cultural relations" are quite horrible to contemplate.

These kinds of considerations may seem vague, speculative, or excessively abstract to some, but it is important that those who concern themselves with culture and the international exchange of ideas understand what, at bottom, cultural relations are all about. No doubt this is somber stuff, but an intelligent acceptance of cultural internationalism requires taking into account its drawbacks as well as its virtues.

4

The Case for Cultural and Informational Programs

AN INTERNATIONALIST public diplomacy has a vital role to play in foreign policy, especially in the emerging post-cold-war era. To arrive at this conclusion requires navigating between two alluring, but false, alternatives: market arguments on behalf of privatization and political rationales for culture and information. Public diplomacy makes good sense, but only from an internationalist perspective that rejects any pretense of promoting national foreign policy interests. In framing the issue in this way, the author runs the risk of sounding like the economist who caused President Truman to dream of finding a one-handed adviser, one who would be unable to say "on the other hand..." But in this area, as in others, there is no way around it. There are no simple answers to complex issues.

Government Sponsorship?

While internationalism today is driven by market forces, reliance on the market alone provides a shaky foundation for a global future. As past experience has demonstrated, it does not have the power by itself to tow either political or cultural internationalism in its wake.

That is because the market thrives only in nurturing political environments, which in turn depend upon internationalist cultural and ideological rationales for their continued existence.

Government does things that the market alone cannot, by intervening where market forces fail to function efficiently. It can reach audiences that private markets cannot and in ways that differ from the methods of the mass media. Driven by fashion and mercurial moods, the market often functions in a notoriously uneven manner, with all kinds of ups, downs and discontinuities. One might even question the degree to which the market ought to function at all in high culture, an area where patronage rather than profit has always been a vital source of income. With all this in mind, it is reasonable to ask whether the private sector is in fact performing adequately in the international cultural and informational arenas.

At a time when foreign policy is more and more swayed by images transmitted instantaneously around the globe, it is foolish to rely solely on the mass media for knowledge of events abroad. Press reports are often sketchy, a problem that is aggravated by the notoriously short attention span of the mass media. Reliance on the media is a poor substitute for the kind of understanding of foreign cultures that comes from study and personal experience. Moreover, far from automatically serving as ambassadors of friendship, the media have often aroused *negative* feelings in much of the world. Even culturally robust countries like France have complained about the penetration of the American media colossus, with its slick images of mindless consumerism, excessive violence and humanistic shallowness. Indeed, one could even argue with some justice that the idea of a two-way flow, with governments serving as traffic cops, is more in keeping with liberal ideals. Allowing the market to operate unchecked is more likely to result in the kind of one-sided cultural imperialism that Third World nations have so harshly criticized.

Ultimately, the market makes for selfish individualism. In its modern form it focuses on promoting an individual consumer consciousness that is far too narrow an outlook to support a sense of international solidarity. Markets may thrive on the basis of individualist sensibilities, but societies cannot. It is one of the ironies of modern politics that those cultural conservatives most often found among right-wing Republicans who mourn the loss of community in the United States tend to be the staunchest advocates of the economic individualism that has been the most potent force in corroding traditional social values.

What holds domestically is all the more true of international society. International commerce has succeeded to a remarkable degree in creating a global society. Unfortunately, it has failed to create, for want of a better term, a global culture. It has certainly contributed to that end, but only in an auxiliary fashion. Commercial internationalism itself has been made possible only as a by-product of this country's conscious commitment, in two world wars and the cold war, to the idea that the world is, in all significant respects, an indivisible whole.

Fulbright Scholarships' Legacy

If the mutual exchange of ideas is desirable, it might help to consider to what extent it would have taken place without cultural and informational programs. Without the Fulbright program, for example, it is doubtful that international awareness, here or abroad, would have approached anywhere near its existing level. By 1988, more than 167,000 Fulbright grantees had received invaluable cultural exposure abroad. Scholarly exchanges would have taken place without Fulbright funding, but on a far smaller scale and in a haphazard manner. While the United States is, by many measures, still a parochial nation, nevertheless it has become less so over the past half century, thanks in significant measure to the Fulbright program.

Similarly, in many areas reached by the information programs, it is not likely that there would have been anywhere near the understanding of the United States that has been attained thanks to their efforts. Although private cultural exchanges dwarf those in the public sphere, nevertheless in relations with developing countries, U.S. support may be crucial to their learning about American society. But the reverse is also true. As historian William McNeill has said, "a wise government and nation ought to support and encourage encounters amongst its citizens with societies in all the world so as to accumulate a stock of knowledge about, and alternate visions of, other peoples and places."

As for waste, the cultural and informational programs have been so small that their inefficiencies pale by comparison to the money spent on other programs. In mid-1993, the overall budget for public diplomacy was less than $1.4 billion. "How little pork, how minute a barrel!" in historian Walter Laqueur's words. Indeed, a single company, Philip Morris, spent more in one year on advertising—$2 billion in 1990—than the combined budgets of all U.S. agencies, official and semiofficial, engaged in public diplomacy. According to Laqueur, "while America spends huge amounts selling cigarettes and soft drinks, it is not selling America."

Part of the problem is that the various programs of public diplomacy have had no powerful constituencies—the major exception being the Fulbright scholars, whose influence appears to be waning. Consequently, the programs are easy marks for politicians who can score cheap symbolic points without offending vested interests. Even though military waste exists on a far greater scale, it generates much less emotional heat because misuse of funds in the cultural programs offers a far safer target for displays of congressional budgetary virtue.

While the effectiveness of cultural relations cannot be measured in statistical terms by bean counters, the marvel is that otherwise hardheaded people are convinced that military expenditures *can* be so calculated, when in fact the overwhelming bulk of them cannot. Historian Chester Pach shows that massive military-aid programs had little in the way of an objective strategic rationale; that is, they contributed nothing demonstrable to the security of America or its allies. These programs were largely symbolic, a reassuring way of telling insecure allies that "we care." At a minimum, cultural and informational programs might be a way of saying the same thing to nations which otherwise might not have very much in common, and at much lower cost. To be sure, military aid has often been profitable for American defense contractors, but that is a very different rationale for the existence of such programs.

Just as there is always friction in mechanics, there is bound to be waste in any governmental activity. Like baseball, in which the best hitters succeed only three times out of ten, some failures can easily be justified. It could be argued that exposing just a few key individuals to American values—in what is inevitably a hit-and-miss operation—might save enormous amounts of money and even men in critical situations. Reaching just one potential leader might well be worth a program. Even individuals who remained unfavorably disposed to the United States after exposure would not be acting wholly on the basis of misinformed conjecture or outright fantasy in the way, say, that Adolf Hitler did in the 1930s. Conflicts born of ignorance are meaningless in a literal sense, whereas struggles over values at least have the potential for dialogue.

Nationalism vs. Internationalism

The tension between informational and cultural programs is likewise a bogus argument against public diplomacy. True, at times the relationship resembled a troubled marriage. But each side also had its advocates of harder or softer approaches. In the informational sphere, for example, there were those who insisted that the United States tell only the whole truth and nothing but, by hewing to the strictest standards of journalistic objectivity and integrity. As President Eisenhower's thinking shows, it was indeed possible to pursue major objectives of U.S. foreign policy through education and exchanges.

Like siblings who have so long been accustomed to fighting with one another that they forget that they belong to the same family, both the cultural and informational programs are embodiments of liberal thought in foreign policy. Just as lobbyists do not necessarily skew the truth and advertisers do not necessarily lie, information is not inherently political nor is it necessarily propaganda. At its best, information seeks to produce understanding, better-informed choices and conflict resolution through the flow of images and ideas, which is exactly what cultural relations seek to produce. All truth begins as local and particularized truth. Arriving at a larger understanding becomes possible only by first digesting and interpreting a myriad of particular truths. Just as lobbyists can be useful sources of information, Public Affairs Officers can help to provide greater detail and understanding abroad about this nation's particular objectives.

By the same token, a culture can never be purely intellectual. It is always connected to social contexts and institutions, and these contain elements of power and interest. Ideas are inevitably attached to this-worldly elements of hierarchy, power and profit. That is why it is impossible to disentangle entirely cultural and commercial internationalism. It follows then, as historian Theodore von Laue has argued in *The World Revolution of Westernization*, that questions of culture are to some extent questions of power. From this point of view, Dulles was quite right to note that Eisenhower's innocent-looking cultural proposals were loaded with political dynamite.

Power politics is itself the product of a belief in the power of culture. For so-called realists, it is precisely cultural differences that make impossible communication in tongues other than the language of power. International conflict is not simply rooted in cultural misperceptions; it stems also from real differences in interests and cultural traditions. And yet, while culture has undeniably been a source of power conflicts, the transfer of ideas and values has also been responsible for global cultural convergence. The growth of cosmopolitanism has never been an automatic process historically destined to end in global harmony. Like all other international values, it has had to be promoted by individuals and by governments, and it has had to be defended, sometimes by force.

All the noisy argumentation about politicization has tended to overlook an important point. If foreign policy is defined in terms of narrow national interests, the goal of universality inevitably becomes a chimera. However, one tends to forget that in the twentieth century, and particularly during the cold war, American foreign policy was committed, in a larger sense, not merely to a national quest for global power but to securing a free global civilization. However recklessly the cold war may have seemed at times to race toward Armageddon, American statesmen never saw the U.S.-Soviet confrontation as merely another instance of selfish and amoral power politics. Instead, the cold war was, in a profound sense, a conflict of contrasting visions of history in which one of the two value systems would inherit the future. It was waged so that the liberal values associated with cultural exchange and free flow of information might not only survive but flourish.

The emphasis placed throughout the struggle on maintaining the allegiance of a favorable world opinion is testimony to the primacy of place that ideas and values held in the thinking of American statesmen. Whatever its paradoxes and imperfections in practice, the American conception of the cold war was intellectually consistent with the liberal sensibility to culture and information. If power could be used without fatal self-contradiction to promote an open world civilization, it stands to reason, then, that cultural and informational programs can play a role in foreign policy without irrevocably compromising their liberal character.

However, that does not mean that these programs ought to operate as a direct appendage of foreign policy. Maintaining their liberal character is absolutely crucial to their effectiveness. Perhaps the issue is best reduced to the question of whether public diplomacy is best suited to a nationalist foreign policy, one that pursues the national interest from a particularist point of view, or whether it is a novel kind of diplomacy that operates best under internationalist assumptions. To date, American policy has sought to combine these two disparate rationales when everything would seem to point to the desirability of jettisoning national-interest justifications.

The Pragmatic Case for Cultural Internationalism

The strongest case for investing in cultural exchanges and engaging in public diplomacy is a pragmatic one that stresses the indispensability of promoting internationalism. To be sure, American values make it difficult to avoid a commitment to openness and a willingness to abide by the results of unforced discussion, or what the contemporary German philosopher Jürgen Habermas has called undistorted communication. But it is not simply a matter of values. No one would advocate a policy of openness if it were wholly useless. It is because its internationalist effectiveness is likely to be hobbled by political distortions, and not for reasons of idealism, that public diplomacy needs to be separated from narrow foreign policy agendas.

But if one is to accept this pragmatic internationalist argument, another needs to be questioned. Though conservatives would disagree, it seems more likely that meaningful cultural *and* informational programs *have* to be internationalist in character and that it is impossible to employ them "realistically" as tools for promoting the national interest. The nationalist belief that they can serve the national interest by promoting narrow foreign policy objectives has been so uncritically accepted that it is not too much to suggest that America's sense of what is practical needs to be turned upside down.

U.S. priorities in the past have been skewed by a misunderstanding of what cultural exchanges and information programs have been about. Cultural policy is a far more serious business than it has been made out to be, while the power of information has been oversold. This outlook has been reflected in the makeup of the USIA, where the informational managers have dominated the agency hierarchy and, on numerous occasions, allowed politics and ideology to dominate their thinking. Just as in the CIA the existence of an "operations mentality" warped what was otherwise a noncontroversial and necessary desire to gain knowledge, in the USIA the informational tail has wagged the cultural dog.

This is not to suggest that the information programs be eliminated in favor of an exclusive emphasis on cultural exchange. As mentioned earlier, there is no natural functional border where one can draw a line between the two. Clearly, many information programs have been useful, though it is precisely when they have been ideologically distorted and made servants of narrow national-interest policies that they have tended to backfire. What is necessary is that the USIA's mission be reconceived from an internationalist point of view. The agency certainly deserves to survive, but it needs more than a reprieve. It needs new life.

It is only when informational and cultural programs are judged by nationalist standards that they appear to be failures. While propaganda and disinformation may produce occasional short-term successes here or there, can lies or deceptions in the service of a short-range national interest really be considered efficacious? These shady practices did the Nazis and the Communists no good in the long run and one could well argue that they were liabilities. Any short-run advantage obtained was unlikely to have materially affected the power equation.

Can other nations or peoples be persuaded to adopt the U.S. view of their national interest? It is doubtful. The assumption underlying the widespread concern with propaganda in the 1930s was that it could be effective in misleading foreign publics. Whatever the validity of that view, a diplomacy of deceit is not open to the United States. Even pushing an honest national point of view too aggressively is likely to raise hackles. At most, information programs can hope to contribute to public debate abroad, to very limited effect. Normally, foreign policy interests are a given, rooted in the historical realities of a nation's situation. If the national interest with regard to any issue is unclear, debate proceeds on the basis of values particular to that nation. This being so, it would be presumptuous to suppose other peoples cannot know or decide their own interest without our help.

If other people do accept the U.S. view of their national interest, it is likely that little or no persuasion was required in the first place. If other nations allow a sympathetic hearing to American information, the battle is, in a sense, won largely before it begins, insofar as the desirability of dialogue is presumed from the start. It is easy to find examples of informational programs that have contributed to foreign policy successes, but it is impossible to prove that those successes would not have occurred without information policy. In sum, the "realistic" approach to information and culture is not as realistic as it pretends to be.

The best to be hoped for is that foreign publics and Americans arrive at an understanding of their *common* interest. In the modern world, agreement or disagreement between peoples cannot be generated by information designed to promote specific policies. Nations can be "penetrated" by media; influentials can be "exposed"; but ultimately the degree of sympathy for the United States generated by information or ideas is a function of ideological compatibility between respective visions of world order. The creation of those larger ideological climates or the capacity to create agreement with them is beyond the reach of any information machine; indeed, it is probably beyond the reach of foreign policy altogether. There are many things in this world that the United States cannot control, and the international climate of opinion is one of them.

Pitfalls of Cultural Nationalism

Other drawbacks of cultural nationalism need also to be taken into account, foremost among them being the conflict that it tends to generate. The resurgence of nationalism in both the North and the South in the second half of this century would seem to suggest that the enthusiasm for cultural internationalism has already peaked. The recent revival of a nostalgic sense of cultural exclusivity, as in the Balkans and the Middle East, might yet be the wave of the future. Sensing such a change in the offing, the political scientist Samuel P. Huntington has suggested that the new post-cold-war era would see the conflict of ideologies replaced by a struggle of civilizations.

Communism may no longer be viable, but these trends suggest that a liberal internationalism dominated by nongovernmental forces will not monopolize the ideological field. Indeed, the post-cold-war era, while less dangerous, is more violent than the period that preceded it. That violence is, to a significant extent, the product of a cultural nationalism that is running rampant in many segments of the world, especially in newly sovereign nations that are desperately in search of identity and cohesion. Even within the relatively cosmopolitan West, there has been a resurgence of belief in ideas that emphasize group singularity and the sacredness of culture. So pronounced are these trends that culture may yet be to the twentieth and twenty-first centuries what nationalism was to the nineteenth: a source of immeasurable conflict.

While cultural chauvinism has been the cause of untold evil and suffering in this world, there are still other unsavory features that come with the particularist outlook. Fashionable as it may be to take the position that "all cultures are created equal," it is only fair to note that there is an elitist and nonegalitarian thrust to such arguments. Just as music critics lament the homogenization of once-unique orchestral sounds in today's orchestras, or critics of cultural imperialism decry the destruction of traditional ways of life, it would be all too easy to fall into a pattern of thought that justifies the separation of endangered cultures, in all their primitive purity, into the equivalent of zoological parks. That kind of cultural argument was in fact used by the South African government to justify its racist policy of *apartheid*.

Understanding Global Interdependence

If the national-interest advantages of informational programs have been exaggerated, the practical arguments on behalf of internationalism have yet to be taken fully to heart. Ultimately, the case for cultural and informational programs is rooted in the need to grapple with the basic paradox of modern interdependence. On the one hand, the globe is now economically, militarily and ecologically interdependent, but it is not yet culturally so. The reality of modernity is that the structural integration of the world has been proceeding more rapidly than its intellectual coordination. Unless a significant amount of cultural integration takes place to match this rapid growth of a global structure, it is not likely that a global society can survive or prosper through technical processes of functional integration alone. Increasingly, understanding will have to direct the unfettered play of market forces. In a functionally interdependent world, the age-old knowledge of power will be overtaken in importance by the power of knowledge.

There would be no urgency to internationalism if interests were in the main local. In that case, it would be mainly of theoretical concern, a hobbyhorse for those given to chasing airy abstractions. However, because American interests depend on a favorable climate of world opinion and an orderly retreat from internationalism is impossible, a compelling argument can be made on behalf of promoting cultural transformation. In case after case in the twentieth century—with respect to military strategy, trade and finance, and environmental issues—thinking about the primacy of the whole over the parts has become a necessity. This has required that Americans transcend their parochial selves by cultivating an international and cosmopolitan dimension to their personalities. Cultural internationalism may be idealistic, but it is no less a historical necessity for that.

It used to be common wisdom that with the Japanese attack on Pearl Harbor in 1941, the American people became instant converts to internationalism. In a national security sense, of course, Americans have indeed become globalists, albeit with great reluctance and, as post-cold-war events would seem to suggest, with a good deal of backsliding. The record of the cold war has shown that cultural and informational policies have been supported only when sold by resort to tough ideological arguments, and genuinely internationalist rationales have often encountered tough sledding. All of this suggests that cosmopolitanism in the United States is still in its infancy and that America is, like other nations, still a very parochial country in many ways. Poor linguistic skills, an often atrocious ignorance of world geography and foreign customs, and an inability to understand imaginatively the problems of others are all indications of a deeply rooted provincial outlook.

But what about the subversive aspects of cultural exchange? How does one justify its undermining of identities? From the larger perspective, cultural relations are aimed as much at changing Americans as at changing others by promoting the worldwide revolution of modernization and modernity. As the literary critic and Palestinian nationalist Edward W. Said has argued, the enormous degree of migration and culture-mixing that takes place in the modern world has made exiles of us all. The exposure to other cultures and value systems, if it produces appreciation and understanding, necessarily casts one's own culture in a new light in which blind patriotism, nationalism and particularism no longer seem so obvious or unquestionably correct. When Senator Fulbright once admitted that his program was intended less to educate outsiders than to educate Americans about the outside world, the light of internationalist wisdom shone through his remarks.

Goals of Internationalism

Internationalism does not aim at the abolition of any nation's culture, which would in any case clearly be impossible. One cannot, for example, expect to create a primary international language. Internationalism aims at something different, a common language of ideology. To be sure, modern ideologies, liberalism included, have penetrated deeper and deeper into what were once the exclusive domains of unique systems of cultural authority. As ideological rationales spell out in ever finer detail how peoples should structure their economies, govern their polities, and define their personal lives, the sphere of culture has begun to retreat into language, literature and the particularity of the national past. Admittedly, then, while internationalism does not abolish culture, it does transform it.

But one should not be so quick to condemn internationalism, for it is doubtful that there has ever existed any such thing as a pure culture. Cultures are human creations that change internally by adaptation and creativity and externally through acculturation. Indeed, one shorthand way of defining *all* human history would be to characterize it as cultural evolution. Throughout history, there have always been imbalances in cultural relationships, and deracination has always, to some extent, been involved. Doing away with cultural and informational programs would not abolish these persistent historical realities.

However nostalgic one may become at the erosion of tradition, there is nothing morally illicit about promoting cultural change. Admittedly, as a matter of principle the shattering of cultural identities is discomfiting, both in what it destroys and in what it creates, especially as there exists no clear idea of what a truly cosmopolitan world would look like. The internationalism of ideas is a form of idealism without utopia, a universalist faith wedded to process rather than to clear goals. But there are values beyond culture, values rooted in the human desire to reach beyond localism and strive for universality. The yearning for truth reflects a need for communication based on standards that transcend the distorted relations that are allied with local and particular interests. Such larger conversations may not be practical in any immediately obvious sense, but the desire to create them speaks volumes about the Enlightenment heritage and its internal logic of rationality and universality.

The issue, therefore, is not really whether government-promoted cultural exchanges are necessary. In today's world, they are, and the need for exchanges will only increase in the course of time. Governments cannot hope to control cultural interactions—that is what cultural policies based on nationalism have sought to do, without much success. What governments *can* do, however, is to promote them, by supplementing the market where necessary and by negotiating the further freeing up of intellectual contact. As was true of the formation of the modern world economy, where governments provided the legal structures, physical security and predictability that nurtured corporate entities, governments today must collectively provide a climate and context in which cultural exchange can take place.

It is understandable that supporters of public diplomacy should wish to find hard, measurable benefits to justify their existence to a skeptical Congress and public. Hence one commonly hears them described as "investments," with the suggestion that there is a bottom-line payoff. Ultimately, though, it seems unlikely that a convincing justification can be found by resorting to cost-accounting techniques. In the author's view, cultural or informational programs cannot effectively promote narrow national interests (of which the United States has many). That sort of thing must be left to the traditional instruments of foreign policy. The programs themselves, like internationalism more generally, are based at bottom on an act of faith, on the assumption that an open and humane world can be constructed through dialogue. Without that assumption, there would be no need for such programs except as outright propaganda. But in that case Washington would be left with power as the only reliable medium for promoting U.S. national interests.

Power is not enough, however. Diplomacy itself was created, after all, out of the need for dialogue, out of the recognition that it was impossible to settle all problems by force, even if nations were disposed to do so. In the past, when dialogue came to an end and diplomatic agreement was impossible, it often made sense to go to war to resolve problems between states. But in the modern era of interdependence, as war has become increasingly too dangerous to contemplate, especially for developed nations, the need for dialogue is all the more pressing. As British Prime Minister Winston Churchill once phrased the alternatives, "to jaw jaw is always better than to war war."

Keeping cultural and informational programs alive is a way of reminding Americans of the basic values of their foreign policy. Although the cultural and informational programs blossomed in the fertile ideological soil of the cold war, the justification for their existence has never been geopolitical in any traditional sense. The disputes about the value of cultural and informational policies are, from this perspective, salutary, for if the United States were to abandon the programs, or stop arguing about them, that would be a sign that U.S. foreign policy had deteriorated to the point that it was concerned solely with power—economic market power if not the military variety. Thus, while cultural and informational policies seek to promote change by creating international understanding, they are also reminders of enduring values that are basic to America's cultural identity. They are a way of remaining true to ourselves.

Talking It Over
A Note for Students and Discussion Groups

This issue of the HEADLINE SERIES, like its predecessors, is published for every serious reader, specialized or not, who takes an interest in the subject. Many of our readers will be in classrooms, seminars or community discussion groups. Particularly with them in mind, we present below some discussion questions—suggested as a starting point only—and references for further reading.

Discussion Questions

Are Americans more sensitive about cultural and informational programs than other peoples? If so, why?

If World War II and the cold war had not taken place, the cultural and informational programs in all likelihood would not have been institutionalized. Does this suggest that the programs were the result of historical contingencies? Or was there some deeper logic underlying their creation?

Is the idea of a democratic propaganda based on a "strategy of truth" self-contradictory? Is it possible to use the concept of freedom as a propaganda theme without at the same time abnegating the values of intellectual freedom?

Are cultural and informational programs essentially different or have the differences between them been exaggerated?

Can cultural and informational programs *successfully* be used in support of realistic foreign policies or, as the author suggests, do they tend to be self-defeating when used in this way?

In what ways exactly are cultural and informational programs related to U.S. foreign policy?

Does the pursuit of cultural internationalism require a utopian act of faith in the oneness of mankind or are there solid practical reasons for advocating cultural internationalism? Are there practical reasons for advocating governmental programs?

Do you agree with the author's argument that market forces alone cannot hold together a global society? Does the market tend to promote individualism, as the author suggests? Why should this be so?

Is cultural internationalism actually anticultural in character? Is a liberal cultural policy an oxymoron?

Is something akin to a "managed free trade" in culture and information preferable, as some Third World nations have suggested?

Do cultural free trade and the free flow of information produce inequities that amount to cultural imperialism? Does exposure to foreign cultures have an impact even on individuals from "sending" cultures? Should the interchange of culture and information be a two-way street?

One feature of American internationalism has been the enduring nationalist belief that Americans have little to learn from foreign cultures in matters of ideology. Is this an example of pure nationalist and ethnocentric logic, or could it be argued that American ideals are universal?

Is culture in any way primordially sacred, as some would have it? The author argues that there is no such thing as a pure culture. Is this true? Why?

Did the cultural programs make a significant contribution to waging the cold war? If so, in what way?

In the last analysis, which programs do you think are more important, the informational or the cultural?

Should the informational and cultural programs be scrapped? continued at present or lower levels of funding? Should the USIA be abolished and its functions shifted to the Department of State? Should it be reorganized?

READING LIST

Alexandre, Laurien, *The Voice of America: From Détente to the Reagan Doctrine*. Norwood, N.J., Ablex Publishing, 1988.

Arndt, Richard T., and Rubin, David Lee, eds., *The Fulbright Difference, 1948–1992*. New Brunswick, N.J., Transaction Publishers, 1993.

Chay, Jongsuk, ed., *Culture and International Relations*. Westport, Conn., Greenwood, 1990.

Coate, Roger A., *Unilateralism, Ideology, & U.S. Foreign Policy: The United States In and Out of UNESCO*. Boulder, Colo., Lynne Rienner, 1988.

Devereux, Anne Rogers, and Seay, George Liston, eds., *Minds Without Borders: Educational & Cultural Exchange in the Twenty-First Century: Fulbright 40th Anniversary Washington Conference Proceeding*. Washington, D.C., USIA, Woodrow Wilson International Center for Scholars and Smithsonian Institution, 1986.

Espinosa, J. Manuel, *Inter-American Beginnings of U.S. Cultural Diplomacy, 1936–1948*. Washington, D.C., USGPO, 1976.

Giffard, C. Anthony, *UNESCO and the Media*. White Plains, N.Y., Longman, 1989.

Hansen, Allen C., *USIA: Public Diplomacy in the Computer Age*. Westport, Conn., Greenwood, 1989.

Hoggart, Richard, *An Idea and Its Servants: UNESCO From Within*. New York, Oxford University Press, 1978.

Horwitz, Richard P., ed., *Exporting America: Essays on American Studies Abroad*. New York, Garland Publishing, 1993.

Johnson, Walter, and Colligan, Francis J., *The Fulbright Program: A History*. Chicago, Ill., University of Chicago Press, 1965.

Kallgren, Joyce, and Simon, Denis Fred, eds., *Educational Exchanges: Essays on the Sino-American Experience*. Berkeley, Calif., Institute of East Asian Studies, 1987.

Lauren, Paul Gordon, *Diplomats and Bureaucrats: The First Institutional Responses to Twentieth-Century Diplomacy in France and Germany*. Stanford, Calif., Hoover Institution Press, 1976.

McMurry, Ruth Emily, and Lee, Muna, *The Cultural Approach: Another Way in International Relations*. Chapel Hill, University of North Carolina Press, 1947.

Mickelson, Sig, *America's Other Voice: The Story of Radio Free Europe and

Radio Liberty. Westport, Conn., Greenwood, 1983.

Mitchell, J.M., *International Cultural Relations*. New York, Unwin Hyman, 1986.

Ninkovich, Frank A., *The Diplomacy of Ideas: U.S. Foreign Policy and Cultural Relations, 1938–1950*. New York, Cambridge University Press, 1981.

Olson, William C., and Howell, Llewellyn D., eds., *International Education: The Unfinished Agenda*. Indianapolis, Ind., White River Press, 1984.

Preston, William, Jr., Herman, Edward S., and Schiller, Herbert I., *Hope & Folly: The United States and UNESCO, 1945–1985*. Minneapolis, University of Minnesota Press, 1989.

Sewell, James P., *UNESCO and World Politics: Engaging in International Relations*. Princeton, N.J., Princeton University Press, 1975.

Tuch, Hans N., *Communicating With the World: U.S. Public Diplomacy Overseas*. New York, St. Martin's Press, 1990.

Tyson, James L., *U.S. International Broadcasting and National Security*. New York, Ramapo Press, 1983.

Wieck, Randolph, *Ignorance Abroad: American Educational and Cultural Foreign Policy and the Office of Assistant Secretary of State*. Westport, Conn., Praeger, 1992.

Statement of Ownership, Management, and Circulation
(Required by 39 U.S.C. 3685)

1. Publication Title: Headline Series
2. Publication No.: 0 1 1 1 - 9 8 1
3. Filing Date: 09/15/95
4. Issue Frequency: Quarterly: Winter, Spring, Summer, Fall
5. No. of Issues Published Annually: 4
6. Annual Subscription Price: $20
7. Complete Mailing Address of Known Office of Publication: Foreign Policy Association 470 Park Ave. South New York, NY 10016-6819
8. Complete Mailing Address of Headquarters or General Business Office of Publisher: Same as above
9. Full Names and Complete Mailing Addresses of Publisher, Editor, and Managing Editor:

Publisher: Foreign Policy Association 470 Park Ave. South New York, NY 10016-6819

Editor: Nancy Hoepli-Phalon 470 Park Ave. South New York, NY 10016-6819

Managing Editor: N/A

10. Owner: Foreign Policy Association, 470 Park Ave. South New York NY 10016-6819

11. Known Bondholders, Mortgagees, and Other Security Holders Owning or Holding 1 Percent or More of Total Amount of Bonds, Mortgages, or Other Securities: N/A

12. For completion by nonprofit organizations: ☒ Has Not Changed During Preceding 12 Months

13. Publication Name: Headline Series
14. Issue Date for Circulation Data Below: Summer 1994

15. Extent and Nature of Circulation	Average No. Copies Each Issue During Preceding 12 Months	Actual No. Copies of Single Issue Published Nearest to Filing Date
a. Total No. Copies (Net Press Run)	8000	8000
b. Paid and/or Requested Circulation (1) Sales Through Dealers and Carriers, Street Vendors, and Counter Sales	778	600
(2) Paid or Requested Mail Subscriptions	1514	1500
c. Total Paid and/or Requested Circulation	2292	2100
d. Free Distribution by Mail	800	700
e. Free Distribution Outside the Mail	0	0
f. Total Free Distribution	800	700
g. Total Distribution	3092	2800
h. Copies Not Distributed (1) Office Use, Leftovers, Spoiled	4908	5200
(2) Return from News Agents	0	0
i. Total	8000	8000
Percent Paid and/or Requested Circulation	74%	75%

16. This Statement of Ownership will be printed in the Fall issue of this publication.

17. Signature and Title of Editor, Publisher, Business Manager, or Owner:  Director of Finance
Date: 09/15/95

PS Form 3526, October 1994